To my mother, Gerri, for her endless love

JANETTA OTTER-BARRY BOOKS

Eye on the Wild: Sea Otter copyright © Frances Lincoln Limited 2013
Text and photographs copyright © Suzi Eszterhas 2013

The right of Suzi Eszterhas to be identified as the author and photographer of this work
has been asserted by her in accordance with the Copyright, Designs and Patents Act,
1988 (United Kingdom).]

First published in Great Britain and in the USA in 2013 by
Frances Lincoln Children's Books, 4 Torriano Mews,
Torriano Avenue, London NW5 2RZ
www.franceslincoln.com

A catalogue record for this book is available from the British Library.

ISBN 978-1-84780-300-9

Set in Stempel Schneidler

Printed in China by C&C Offset Printing Co., Ltd in November 2012

1 3 5 7 9 8 6 4 2

SEA OTTER

Suzi Eszterhas

F

FRANCES LINCOLN
CHILDREN'S BOOKS

Far away, in the cool waters of the Pacific Ocean, a baby sea otter is born. The tiny ball of fluff is just a little bigger than a kitten and is as sweet as can be. She snoozes in the sushine, safe and secure on her mother's warm, cozy belly.

The baby sea otter is very lucky. Mom gives her lots of hugs and constant love and attention. Mom's job for the next six months is to teach the little pup how to find food and look after herself, and to keep her spotlessly clean. But the pup gets very tired and sleeps for most of the day.

The otter pup has the warmest fur coat in the world. Her fur is so fluffy and thick that it keeps her from sinking underwater. So when Mom goes diving for food, the pup floats on top of the water like a cork. This keeps the pup safe from drowning, until she gets a little older and can learn how to swim.

The pup is always hungry. She spends hours lying on Mom's tummy, drinking lots of rich milk. This will help her to grow big and strong, very fast. While the pup is busy drinking, Mom cleans her. She blows air bubbles into the little otter's fur to keep her warm and dry.

If Mom is in a hurry, or danger threatens,
she gently carries the pup in her mouth –
just as a mother cat carries her kitten. Kicking
her powerful back feet, she speeds through
the water to take her baby to a safer place.

By the time the pup is three months old, she has learned how to swim. But Mom always stays close by to protect her. If a strange otter gets too close, the pup gets frightened and jumps on to Mom's back. Mom then makes a scary face and rushes at the other otter. There's a lot of chasing and splashing, and the pup has to hold on tightly or she will fall off.

The pup's next lesson is a tricky one. She has to learn how to dive and find food. Clams and crabs are her favorite snacks – she wants to eat them all the time – but it takes months for her to learn how to find them on their own. Luckily, Mom is always happy to share her catch – and her chest makes a great table to eat on.

After about four months, the pup is diving on her own. But Mom is always careful to make sure she knows exactly where she is. If the pup ever gets lost, Mom gives a very loud squeal. The pup knows the sound of Mom's call and answers back right away, so they can find each other quickly.

When the otter pup is just six months old she is nearly as big as Mom. She's not quite grown-up yet, but it is time for her to explore the ocean world on her own. At last, she can try all the things Mom has taught her – like finding food, keeping warm, and staying out of danger.

The pup sets off on her big adventure and begins to explore the world all by herself. She swims along the coast, and even comes out of the water to look at rockpools and warm, sandy beaches. She's a bit clumsy on land at first, but soon learns to use her webbed feet to stroll up and down the shore.

Soon the young otter finds a group of other otters floating together – and she makes some new friends. These groups of otters are called 'rafts' and sometimes there can be hundreds of otters in just one raft. The otters look out for each other, and shout a warning if danger comes near.

It can be very cold in the sea and the otter does not have much fat to keep her warm. Instead she has a very thick fur coat. But she has to keep her coat spotlessly clean to stay warm and healthy, and spends a lot of time grooming – just as her mom taught her.

The young sea otter loves to
snooze in the sun. She can't wear
sunglasses, of course, so when
the sun is too bright she uses
her soft paws to cover her eyes.
Sometimes she falls into a deep
sleep like this but, luckily,
her thick fur stops her
from getting sunburned.

Finding food is not always easy. The otter uses her long whiskers to feel for crabs and clams in the dark depths of the ocean. She also carries a rock in a special fur pocket, just under her arm. This rock makes the perfect tool – like a hammer – for breaking open the hard shells of crabs and clams.

Diving for food is hard work, so sometimes the young otter takes a well-earned break. She finds a nice bed of kelp or sea-grass, wraps it around her body to make sure she doesn't drift out to sea, and then falls into a lovely deep sleep.

On her first birthday, the otter has finally grown up. Mom taught her well and she feels safe and at home in the ocean. She knows how to swim fast, dive deep, find food, and stay warm. Soon she will be able to ride the waves with her own baby curled up, fast asleep, on her warm furry tummy.

More about Sea Otters

- Sea otters live on the coasts of California, Washington, Alaska, Canada, Russia, and Japan.

- Sea otters' fur has over one million hairs per square inch, the thickest fur of any animal in the world.

- Sea otters are bigger than they look. They are the size of German Shepherd dogs, weighing 45–90 pounds.

- Sea otters have very high metabolisms and must eat about 25% of their weight in food each day to survive. Sea otters eat sea urchins, abalone, mussels, clams, crabs, snails and about 40 other marine species.

- Sea otters use tools. They use small rocks or other objects to pry shellfish from rocks and to hammer them open. Some otters have taken to using Coke bottles as tools.

- A sea otter's coat has pockets – flaps of skin under each front leg. An otter uses them to stash its tools or prey during a dive, which leaves its paws free to hunt some more.

- Sea otters can dive over 300 feet deep and can hold their breath for almost five minutes.

- Sea otters are endangered because people used to hunt them for their fur and people are now destroying their ocean home.

- For more information www.seaotters.com